Melanie

A One-Of-A-Kind
Hot Air Balloon
ADVENTURE

www.uncledavesbooks.com

Published by Uncle Dave's Books
www.uncledavesbooks.com
Books are doors into imagination
Book design copyright © 2017 by Uncle Dave's Books.
All rights reserved.
Cover and interior design by Eileen Cueno
Illustrations by Francis Eugene Veloso

UncleDavesBooks.com

Published in the United States of America

ISBN: 978-0-692-84581-3
1. Juvenile Fiction / Action & Adventure / General
2. Juvenile Fiction / Humorous Stories

THIS BOOK BELONGS TO:

_____

Get carried
away!

Melanie♡

"This is a one-of-a-kind hot air balloon," Uncle Ezra said.

The three of us—Uncle Ezra, my brother Andy, and I—were in the backyard in the basket ready for takeoff.

"Uh-oh!" Uncle Ezra said, jumping out of the basket. He ran toward the house. "Nature calls. Bathroom break!"

Andy and I looked at each other. I climbed out of the basket to stretch my legs.

"What's this?" Andy said.

I heard a loud hiss and looked up to see Andy pulling a cord. Fire shot up into the balloon. It started to rise off the ground.

"Wait for me!" I shouted. "You don't know what you're doing."

"Neither do you," he shouted back.

I grabbed hold of the basket before it could lift in the air, out of reach.

We were both shouting for help, and I was swinging my feet over the side of the basket when Farmer Brian next door heard our cries and chased after us. He grabbed my braids and held on before the balloon lifted too high. The balloon kept rising. It lifted him off the ground with us.

A little girl was walking her puppy down a country road.

"Help!" we all shouted.

The little girl grabbed hold of Farmer Brian's boots. Her puppy, not wanting to be left out, jumped up and bit the little girl's pant leg and held on with his teeth.

We sailed over fields of corn and sunflowers, inching higher and higher off the ground.

A big round lady came bouncing out of her house to see what the matter was.

"I can help!" she said.

She took hold of the puppy's tail. But instead of bringing everyone safely back down, the balloon lifted her up into the air too.

We were floating through the countryside with the round lady creeping higher in the air when a van full of tourists drove up.

"Help! Help!" we all shouted.

"Take hold of our antenna and we'll pull you back down," the driver said.

The round lady gripped the van's antennae with one hand and the puppy's tail in the other. We headed into town that way, my brother and me, Farmer Brian, the girl and her puppy, the round lady, and the vanload of tourists, when the van began to rise off the ground too.

We headed right for the zoo and flew over the monkey enclosure.

The biggest monkey latched hold of the van's bumper, and all the monkeys began to clasp hands and climb out of the enclosure to join us. One by one they locked arms right down to the littlest monkey.

All together the balloon picked up and carried away twenty-seven monkeys.

We moved over the harbor and out to sea, all of us screaming and squealing and barking and honking and screeching. Then a tugboat captain blasted over her megaphone, "We'll save you!"

She steered the boat below our balloon and picked up a rope. She lassoed the pinky toe of the last little monkey. Then she tied the rope to the boat rail.

But just as the tugboat began tugging us safely in, it started to lift off the water and float up through the sky with us.

We rose higher and higher, up through the clouds and then above them.

An airplane flew by. All the passengers in the airplane stared and waved. I could only smile and not wave back because both of my hands were holding tight to the basket.

We continued up and up, through the atmosphere, right into space.

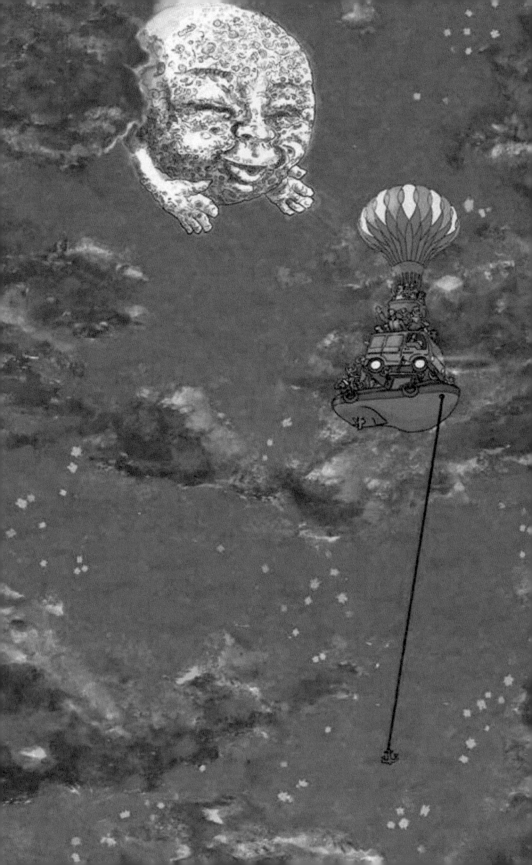

As we floated by, the man in the moon tried to grab hold of us to help. But having small hands, he couldn't.

"Sorry," he cried as we sailed past.

We were heading straight toward the sun.

"We will all be burnt up like toast!" cried the little girl.

Then Andy said, "I know what to do. There's a slingshot in my pocket. I could shoot the balloon with it and send us back down to earth."

"Nooo!" everyone screamed at once.

But it was too late. He took his hands off the cord and searched around in his pocket for his sling.

When he did, the fire stopped shooting into the balloon. The balloon with Andy and me, Farmer Brian, the little girl and her puppy, the round lady, the van full of tourists, the twenty-seven monkeys, and the tugboat all started to sink back down, past the moon, toward the earth, down below the airplane and its passengers, below the clouds and over the sea.

"Oh!" Andy said. "So that's how it works."

"Do you mean that all you had to do was take your hands off the cord at any time and we would have gone back down?" I yelled.

"I guess so," he said.

Soon we were over the harbor again.

The tugboat captain let go of the littlest monkey's toe with her lasso and gently touched her boat down.

Then we were over the monkey enclosure at the zoo. Each monkey from littlest to the biggest hopped safely back into the enclosure.

That's the way it continued until everyone was returned safely to the ground where he or she belonged.

We touched down in the backyard when Uncle Ezra came rushing out of the house.

"Who's ready for a one-of-a-kind hot air balloon ride?" he asked.

"I think we changed our minds," said Andy.

"Yeah," I agreed. "Let's take a train ride instead."

Here is the true story of another one-of-a-kind hot air balloon adventure...

Since the beginning of time people have dreamed of flying. When it was discovered that hot air trapped in a balloon would make the balloon rise off the ground and float through the air, it wasn't long before people wanted to test that idea to see if it could help them reach their goal of flying.

On September 19th, 1783 the people of Versailles, France lined up in the palace courtyard. They watched as a sheep, a duck and a rooster were loaded into a hot air balloon basket. The hot air balloon with the barnyard trio tucked inside the basket set sail over the skies of Versailles. It traveled 5.5 miles in 8 minutes and touched down in a nearby woods outside of the city.

A newspaper at the time wrote, "It was judged that they [the sheep, the duck and the rooster] had not suffered, but they were, to say the least, much astonished."

A few months later a teacher and a soldier both took off in their balloon not far away in Paris, France. They floated 6 miles in 25 minutes. Benjamin Franklin, one of the Founding Fathers of the United States, was one of the spectators this time and wrote about it in his journal, "We observed [the balloon] lift off in the most majestic manner...We could not help feeling a certain mixture of awe and admiration."

Hot air balloons are simple flying machines and are made up of three components (parts):

1. an envelope
2. burners
3. basket

MAYA

ANDY

UncleDavesBooks.com

Made in the USA
Columbia, SC
10 March 2022